The Martian Principles

Principles

for Successful
Enterprise Systems

20 Lessons Learned
from NASA's Mars Exploration
Rover Mission

Ronald Mak

WILEY

Wiley Publishing, Inc.

The Martian Principles for Successful Enterprise Systems

Published by
Wiley Publishing, Inc.
10475 Crosspoint Boulevard
Indianapolis, IN 46256
www.wiley.com

Published by Wiley Publishing, Inc., Indianapolis, Indiana

Published simultaneously in Canada

ISBN-13: 978-0-471-78965-9
ISBN-10: 0-471-78965-8

Manufactured in the United States of America

10 9 8 7 6 5 4 3 2 1

1B/RX/QU/QW/IN

For general information on our other products and services or to obtain technical support, please contact our Customer Care Department within the U.S. at (800) 762-2974, outside the U.S. at (317) 572-3993 or fax (317) 572-4002.

Wiley also publishes its books in a variety of electronic formats. Some content that appears in print may not be available in electronic books.

Library of Congress Cataloging-in-Publication Data
Mak, Ronald, 1953-
    The Martian principles for successful enterprise systems : 20 lessons learned from NASA's Mars Exploration Rover Mission / Ronald L. Mak.
        p. cm.
    Includes index.
    ISBN-13: 978-0-471-78965-9 (pbk.)
    ISBN-10: 0-471-78965-8 (pbk.)
    1. Mars Exploration Rover Mission (U.S.)—Data processing. 2. Computer systems—Design—Case studies. 3. Business—Data processing—Case studies. 4. Mars (Planet)—Exploration—Data processing. 5. Roving vehicles (Astronautics)—Automatic control—Data processing. I. Mars Exploration Rover Mission (U.S.) II. Title.
    TL799.M3M35 2006
    658'.05—dc22
                    2006003347

Wiley also publishes its books in a variety of electronic formats. Some content that appears in print may not be available in electronic books.

About the Author

Ronald Mak was a senior computer scientist and software architect at the NASA Ames Research Center. He was the architect and lead developer of the middleware for the Collaborative Information Portal, an important enterprise software system that is a part of NASA's ongoing and highly successful Mars Exploration Rover mission. Mission managers, scientists, and engineers continue to use CIP—after over two years of continuous operation, it has an uptime record of better than 99.9 percent. Working as a key member of the CIP development team validated the principles that Ron describes in this book.

Ron was also the architect and lead developer of an enterprise-class information portal for NASA's International Space Station and the future Crew Exploration Vehicle.

Prior to joining NASA, Ron had over 15 years of experience designing and developing enterprise systems using several programming languages and technologies on various platforms. Most of these systems were highly successful, but there were a few failures, too. The Martian principles are derived from these experiences.

Ron held an academic appointment with the University of California at Santa Cruz, and he worked on contract to NASA

Ames. He earned his B.S. degree with distinction in the Mathematical Sciences and his M.S. degree in Computer Science from Stanford University. He has written three previous books on computer science, *Java Number Cruncher, the Java Programmer's Guide to Numerical Computing* (Prentice Hall PTR, 2003), *Writing Compilers and Interpreters, C++ Edition* (Wiley, 1996), and *Writing Compilers and Interpreters, a Practical Approach* (Wiley, 1991). He recently wrote several papers about CIP for refereed journals. He continues to hone his exposition of the Martian principles by giving presentations to both industry and academic audiences.

Ron recently co-founded and is the CTO of Willard & Lowe Systems, Inc. (www.willardlowe.com) which develops enterprise systems for information management and collaboration.

Credits

Executive Editor
Carol Long

Development Editor
Keith Cline

Production Editor
Felicia Robinson

Copy Editor
Foxxe Editorial Services

Editorial Manager
Mary Beth Wakefield

Production Manager
Tim Tate

**Vice President and
Executive Group Publisher**
Richard Swadley

**Vice President and
Executive Publisher**
Joseph B. Wikert

Project Coordinator
Michael Kruzil

**Graphics and
Production Specialists**
Beth Brooks
Stephanie D. Jumper

Quality Control Technician
Brian H. Walls

Proofreading and Indexing
Laura L. Bowman
Stephen Ingle

Contents

Preface

When I was growing up, I wanted to be an astronaut. The Space Race was on, and men were walking on the moon. What could be more exciting for a kid?

I was inspired to study science and mathematics, and later, while still in junior high school, I became an early nerd and fell in with computers. Eventually, I grew up and went to university to earn my degrees in mathematics and in computer science. Alas, by then, men were no longer walking on the moon.

Since then, I have been working in Silicon Valley as a successful software developer, architect, and engineering manager, in both established companies and in start-ups. I designed, programmed, and led the development of applications, graphical user interfaces, compilers, numerical utilities, windowing systems, and distributed systems on a variety of platforms. As the Internet and the World Wide Web become dominant environments, I settled into designing and developing enterprise software systems.

In late 2001, I had a chance meeting with an old university classmate who was working at the NASA Ames Research Center located south of San Francisco. He was a member of a team developing an enterprise system for an upcoming space mission, and he mentioned to me that they were looking for an enterprise architect.

In March 2002, I started working at NASA Ames. I was indeed fortunate to join the software team that was developing the Collaborative Information Portal, or CIP, an Internet-based enterprise information system for the Mars Exploration Rover (MER) mission. I became the architect and the lead developer for CIP's middleware infrastructure as part of an extremely hard-working team that had real deadlines to meet. The rovers were scheduled to launch in June and July 2003, and they were going to land on Mars in January 2004. The software for the mission had to be ready on time, or it simply wasn't going to be included. At NASA, the term *launch window* for a product has more than one meaning!

Now fast forward to the present. Both rovers landed successfully, and they have performed their scientific tasks superbly beyond anyone's expectations. The mission was only supposed to last 90 Earth days, but as of the end of December 2005, after nearly two Earth years, they continue to operate.

Much of the mission software has been equally impressive. In particular, since becoming operational in December 2003, the month before the rovers landed on Mars, CIP has been fulfilling its tasks faithfully and reliably, and it has maintained better than a 99.9 percent uptime record. It handles major spikes in usage whenever some interesting data or image downloaded by one of the rovers first becomes available. CIP now runs continuously several months at a time without interruption, and it goes down completely only for hardware or network maintenance. The success and reliability of CIP are due to many key design principles we followed throughout the enterprise system. In this book, I hope to convey, from my perspective as a middleware architect, what some of these principles are. I draw upon all of my experience, both at NASA and from before, but I use CIP to illustrate the principles.

Inspiration and Hope for This Book

Designing and developing the CIP middleware was the culmination of my years of experience with distributed applications and enterprise software systems. When I joined the project in March 2002 as its middleware architect, I needed to design and develop a new middleware infrastructure. The mission's next major Operational Readiness Test at JPL was four months away. The rovers were going to launch in a little more than a year, and code freeze was scheduled for November 2003. CIP would become operational in December 2003. So when I started, we needed an operational prototype in four months, and we had about 20 months to get the final version designed, developed, debugged, and deployed. I knew I had very little room for error—the middleware could either pull the entire development project forward toward a successful completion, or it could become the developmental bottleneck that dragged the project down.

Working on CIP crystallized and validated the principles I had been formulating during my professional career. Hence, I call them the Martian principles in this book, where I enumerate and describe these principles and their corollaries. In Part 1, I inserted "Mission Notes" that provide specific examples or anecdotes from the CIP project to help illustrate and clarify the principles.

Because I was the middleware architect for CIP—and I had similar roles before I started to work at NASA—I wrote this book from the middleware architect's point of view. I hope that does not diminish its usefulness for readers who have other roles. Whenever I use the word "you," I want it to refer to all enterprise system architects, developers, and project managers.

I based this book on two classics I've read: *The Elements of Style* by William Strunk, Jr. and E. B. White; and *The Elements of Programming Style* by Brian W. Kernighan and P. J. Plauger.

The former is about writing English prose, and the latter is about writing computer programs. Both books are short. Each enumerates and briefly explains a small number of key principles in plain, simple language.

I remember my thought progression when I first read these books, especially the one on programming. "I'm already a good programmer, so I don't really need to read this book," I thought. As I read some of the principles, I would say to myself, "Well, *of course!* This is just so much common sense. For sure, that's how I do it!" Then later I would equivocate, "Okay, Okay, I know I really *should* do it that way." Upon some reflection after I finished reading the book, I had to admit that I really did learn some new things and that my software development skills would improve because of that.

I can only aspire to be as good a writer as the authors of those two books. Nevertheless, I hope you will have the same favorable reactions from reading this book, and that the Martian principles will help you make your enterprise projects succeed. Yes, most of it seems to be just plain common sense. But too often, I'm surprised by how *uncommon* common sense can be.

For More Information

You can find more information about the ongoing Mars Exploration Rover mission at the official MER mission website, http://marsrovers.jpl.nasa.gov/home/index.html.

For a more comprehensive overview of the CIP, read the article "The Collaborative Information Portal and NASA's Mars Rover Mission" by Ronald Mak and Joan Walton in the January-February 2005 issue of *IEEE Internet Computing*, volume 9, number 1, pages 20–26.

Contact Information

I will post the latest information about this book to my website,
`http://www.apropos-logic.com`.

You can write to me at `ron@apropos-logic.com`.

Disclaimer

All the opinions I express in this book are my own and not necessarily those of any other CIP or MER project members, NASA, or the University of California. Any mention of commercial products is not an endorsement by NASA or the University of California.

Ronald Mak
San José, California

Acknowledgments

Much of the credit for the overwhelming success of the MER mission goes to the mission managers, scientists, and engineers at the Jet Propulsion Laboratory (JPL). They landed not one, but two rovers on Mars, and both robotic geologists have returned large amounts of invaluable scientific data. We were all privileged to work with them.

CIP could not have been developed without a dedicated team with project members from both Ames and JPL. The team members included, in alphabetical order, Roy Britten, Louise Chan, Sanjay Desai, Matt D'Ortenzio, Glen Elliott, Robert Filman, Dennis Heher, Kim Hubbard, Sandra Johan, Leslie Keely, Carson Little, Vish Magapu, Quit Nguyen, Tarang Patel, John Schreiner, Jeff Shapiro, Elias Sinderson, Joan Walton, Bob Wing, and myself. This team worked as though it were at a start-up.

I thank my development editor at Wiley, Keith Cline, for much encouragement, guidance, and virtual hand-holding. Executive editor Carol Long took some of my initial half-baked ideas and turned them into a vision for a book. My agent, William Brown of Waterside Productions, did all the important work to get me a book contract to sign.

Introduction

What Do Martians Know about Enterprise Systems?

Most enterprise software systems are not successful. They either fail outright, or they become operational despite significant unmet requirements. If you are designing, developing, and deploying an enterprise system, the odds are stacked against you.

This may be discouraging if you have never designed or built such a system before. If you have tried, whether successfully or not, you may have been amazed by how difficult it turned out to be.

So, why is it so hard to create a successful enterprise system? After all, aren't there industry standards that govern how to design and build the components? Certainly, there are now tons of "how to" and "for dummies" books on the subject. And what about all those expensive developers' tools and utilities that promise to crank out all the code for you? Hey, just enter your parameter values, drag this here and drop that there, push the green button, do not look behind the curtain—*et voilà!*—out comes your Enterprise System Deluxe, all debugged and ready to roll. What's the big deal?

I believe that many enterprise development projects ultimately fail because they start off on the wrong track. At the beginning, the project managers and the developers emphasize the wrong things, such as how to write the code and which development tools to use. Indeed, early management and design decisions often revolve around coding and tools.

However, enterprise projects, even the more complex ones, can succeed if they adhere to certain principles. This book enumerates and explains some of these key principles.

These principles exist on a higher plane than coding or tools—they are not coding examples, and they do not prescribe which tools to use. The principles are not design patterns (although one of the principles strongly advises using design patterns). Instead, these principles help the project team members, whether architects, programmers, or project managers, get into the right mindset to ensure success. They apply equally well to any of the current enterprise technologies, such as Java 2 Enterprise Edition (J2EE), .NET, or Common Object Request Broker Architecture (CORBA). These principles provide high-level guidance to set the right priorities and to put the focus on what is really important.

Where do these principles come from? They emerged from my more than 20 years of experience designing, developing, and managing distributed applications and enterprise software projects. I've seen successes and a few failures. My most recent experience—fortunately, it was a great success—was being the architect and lead developer of the middleware for the Collaborative Information Portal (CIP) that is used by NASA's Mars Exploration Rover mission.

The Mars Exploration Rover Mission

NASA's Mars Exploration Rover (MER) mission launched two robotic geologists, named Spirit and Opportunity, to Mars in June and July 2003. Mission control was, and continues to be, at

NASA's Jet Propulsion Laboratory (JPL) located near Los Angeles. The rovers landed triumphantly on January 3 and January 24, 2004 on opposite sides of Mars, Spirit in Gusev Crater and Opportunity in Meridiani Planum. Each rover, about the size of a golf cart, was to spend 90 Earth days roving and analyzing its surroundings in search of evidence that liquid water covered parts of the Martian surface in the past and whether there once was life.

Each rover is equipped with a number of cameras and scientific instruments, including a rock abrasion tool for drilling into surfaces, a microscopic imager, and several spectrometers. Most of the instruments are deployed on a flexible arm (see Figure I-1). The rovers are solar powered, and because they landed on opposite sides of the planet, there is always one of them active in sunlight.

The rovers have been extremely successful, way beyond anyone's original expectations. Instead of only 90 Earth days, as of late December 2005, they have continued to operate and send back valuable data and images for nearly two Earth years (and over one Martian year). Based on these data and images, scientists on Earth have concluded that liquid water did indeed once cover parts of the surface of Mars. Each rover has traveled nearly four miles, including climbing up the sides of craters.

Depending on their relative positions, it takes anywhere from about 4 minutes to about 20 minutes for a radioed command signal to go from Earth to Mars, and double that time for a command-response signal round trip. Therefore, we cannot control the rovers "by joystick." Instead, the rovers are semi-autonomous; scientists on Earth construct and send a separate command sequence to each rover. The rover obeys the commands but can react by itself to local conditions and hazards.

Each rover is controlled by a radiation-hardened version of the PowerPC chip operating at 20 million instructions per second. Onboard memory is 128 MB of RAM, augmented by 256 MB of nonvolatile flash memory.

Figure I-1: An artist's depiction of a rover working on Mars. The flexible arm mounted with scientific instruments is approaching a rock to analyze. *Image courtesy of NASA/JPL-Caltech.*

The Collaborative Information Portal

Beginning a few years before the rovers landed on Mars, the MER mission managers at JPL worked closely with a small software development team at the NASA Ames Research Center located south of San Francisco. The goal was to develop the Collaborative Information Portal (CIP) for the mission that would meet several major requirements:

- **User management** includes managing user accounts and access privileges—in other words, user authentication (do you have a valid user ID and password?) and authorization (are you allowed to see this data?). Users also need to work together and share their results.

- **Time synchronization** is important because during the first several months, the mission ran on Mars time. Each Martian day, or "sol," is nearly 40 minutes longer than an Earth day, so the people who work on Mars time shift that amount of time each day relative to everyone else who is on Earth time. Also, there are two Martian time zones, one per rover, and various Earth time zones, since the mission has collaborators throughout the United States and other parts of the world. It is vital to keep everybody on the mission synchronized, especially when there are two separate rover teams working.

- **Data access** is critical in a mission that involves much data and many images of various types and formats downloaded to Earth by two rovers analyzing two completely different locations on Mars. Mission engineers process the downloaded data and images and store them into the mission file server. Of course, the scientists all want access to these files as soon as they are available, and they also need to access archived information. There are security restrictions on some of the files, and access to them is limited only to users with the proper clearances and privileges.

- **Scheduling** is challenging in an environment where two teams of mission managers, scientists, and engineers are working strange hours around the Martian clock with two separate rovers. People working in different roles have different needs, and some people have changing roles during the course of a sol. Each person needs to know with whom he or she should be working, and where that person is located. Managers and their subordinates need to communicate with each other. Needless to say, staff scheduling is complex in such an environment.

To meet these mission requirements, CIP is a major enterprise system that enables MER mission managers and the scientists, researchers, and engineers to access mission information securely over the Internet. This information includes the following:

- The data and image files downloaded by the rovers on Mars and then processed and stored into the mission file server.
- The current time in various Earth and Mars time zones.
- Event and personnel schedules.
- Text messages sent by users.

CIP provides *situational awareness*. CIP also enables user collaboration by allowing users to make annotations and comments about the files, which are then shared with other users who access the files.

Each user sees CIP as a collection of useful tools that provide these capabilities. Figure I-2 is a screen shot of several of these tools. Figure I-3 is a screen shot of the Data Products Browser tool. A "data product" is a file containing data generated by a rover instrument or an image taken by a rover camera that had been downloaded to Earth, processed by the JPL engineers, and stored into the mission file server. CIP generates metadata about each data product so that it can categorize them by sol, rover, and instrument. Users can conduct sophisticated searches based on metadata fields.

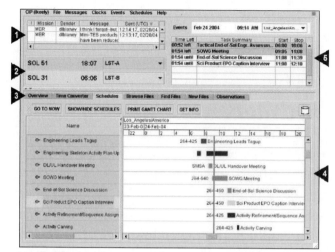

Figure I-2: A screen shot of some of the CIP client tools: (1) broadcast messages, (2) clocks displaying the current time in various time zones on Earth and Mars, (3) tool tabs to access other client tools, (4) schedule viewer, and (5) event horizon displaying starting time countdowns of user-selected scheduled events.

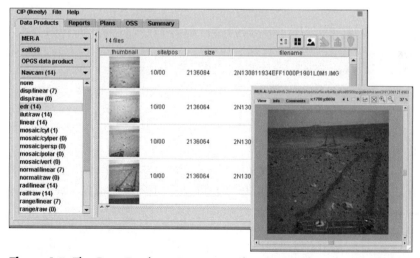

Figure I-3: The Data Products Browser and an image downloaded from the mission file server to the user's workstation or laptop.

Image courtesy of NASA/JPL-Caltech.

Software Architecture

Architecture refers to how something was constructed. We commonly talk about a building's architecture.

A building may have multiple architectures, depending on your point of view. For example, if you walked in front of an office building, you would notice the architecture of the building's exterior, including its shape, its façade, and the placement of the doors and windows. But if you worked inside that building, your view of the architecture would include the layout of its interior and the sizes and shapes of its rooms. If, however, you were a plumber or electrician, you would have an altogether different idea of the building's architecture.

Software architecture is similar. It depends on your point of view.

A CIP user sees the graphical user interface (GUI) of the client tools, examples of which are shown in Figures I-2 and I-3. There are fixed elements, such as windows, frames, and text labels. There are displays of dynamic information, such as time, schedules, data, and images. There are also user input elements such as buttons, tabs, and menus that enable the user to send commands to CIP.

What the CIP user sees is the *Model-View-Controller* (MVC) architecture. The view is the display of the dynamic information, and the controller consists of the buttons, tabs, and menus. The model is the information and associated processing logic that is somewhere "out there" beyond the GUI—the user does not really have to know where.

The key idea behind the MVC architecture is that the model, view, and controller are functionally separate parts of the system. The user sends commands via the controller. These commands may modify the view directly, or they may tell the model to alter its state. The altered model then updates how the view displays parts of the model's data. The user may react to changes in the view by interacting with the controller to send new commands. The user never manipulates the model directly, only through the controller. Figure I-4 is a diagram of this architecture.

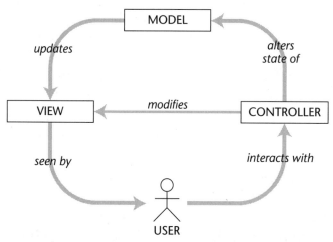

Figure I-4: The Model-View-Controller (MVC) architecture.

From functional point of view, CIP has a prototypical *Service-Oriented Architecture* (SOA). In an SOA, a central server provides services to client applications. A client sends a request to a service, and the service returns a response. To formulate this response, the service may itself send requests to other services, or it may access data from the back-end databases, file servers, and other data sources. The collection of services makes up what is commonly known as *middleware*, because it sits between the users' client applications and the data sources. (The term *SOA* was not in vogue at the beginning of the CIP development project. When the term became more common, we realized that was indeed what we were building.)

Service requests and responses are typically done with an industry standard called *web services*. There are several popular ways to implement the middleware services themselves. As the middleware architect, I chose to design CIP's middleware infrastructure around the Java-based J2EE standard.

Web services use a protocol called the Simple Object Access Protocol (SOAP), and because the protocol is based on Extensible Markup Language (XML), it is both programming language- and platform-independent. The CIP middleware services support the CIP client tools, which are written in Java. They also support other client applications written in C++. Each service expects to be sent properly formulated SOAP requests, and it returns properly formulated SOAP responses. Each client tool or application relies upon a standard library specific to its language to convert the requests and responses between the language and SOAP. Similarly, each middleware service uses a Java package to convert the requests and responses between the Java language and SOAP.

The CIP middleware provides a number of services that the CIP client tools and other client applications share. Each client tool or application may send requests to one or more services in any combination. The services include the following:

- **User management service** to maintain user accounts, manage user sessions, and to perform user authentication and authorization.

- **Metadata service** to use the metadata about the data and image files in the mission file server to categorize the data products, access each product, and enable sophisticated product searches.

- **Schedule service** to store, update, and access personnel and event schedules.

- **Time service** to maintain the current time in various Mars and Earth time zones, and to convert times between different time zones.

- **Streamer service** to upload and download (i.e., stream) data between the client applications and the mission file server, and to create trees that represent the file server's directory hierarchies.

- **Message service** to handle asynchronous and synchronous messaging.

From an organizational point of view, CIP has a *three-tiered enterprise architecture*, as shown in Figure I-5:

- **Client tier** contains all the remote client applications, such as the CIP client tools shown in Figures I-2 and I-3.

- **Middleware tier** contains all the services. The CIP middleware tier runs the services in an application server, which also provides support for the web services.

- **Data tier**, also known as the back end, includes all of the data sources, such as the CIP metadatabase and the mission file server. Included in this tier are the back-end data acquisition utility programs.

As I mentioned earlier, I designed the CIP middleware around the J2EE standard. We implemented the services with Enterprise JavaBeans (EJB). Some of the EJBs are *service providers*, and each one is an interface to a web service. Other EJBs are *business objects* that perform the processing logic of the services. Some of them access the data sources in the data tier. All the EJBs operate in a runtime environment called an *application server*. I chose the commercial WebLogic application server from BEA Systems, Inc.

We configured CIP's web services to pass encrypted data and commands through the mission firewalls.

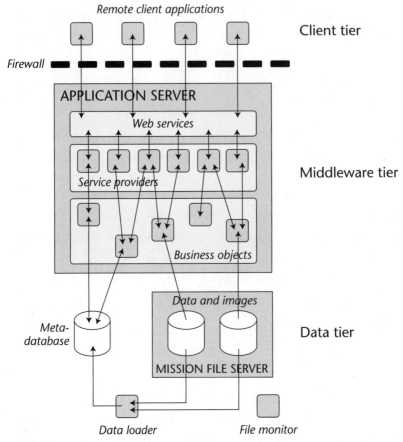

Figure I-5: The three-tiered enterprise architecture.

Figure I-5 shows two CIP data acquisition utility programs in the data tier. The file monitor watches the mission file server for any newly created or updated files. The data loader generates metadata for each file which it loads into the metadatabase. This metadata is used by several client tools such as the Data Products Browser shown in Figure I-3.

The various architectural views are interrelated, just as a building's internal architecture is related to its external architecture. The middleware and data tiers of CIP's enterprise architecture make up the model part of the MVC architecture. These two tiers also constitute the central server of the SOA that responds to service requests.

Finally, from a software developer's point of view, we built CIP using a *component-based architecture*. Components are software units, such as Java classes, that implement a standard interface. From Figure I-5, it is clear that the middleware is composed of the EJB components, each of which implements an interface defined by the J2EE standard. The CIP client tools are also component-based. We built their GUI using Java Swing components such as windows, panels, text labels, buttons, and menus. Each component implements a standard Swing interface.

A component-based architecture enforces code modularity. Because the components implement well-defined standard interfaces, they are easier to develop and debug. The architecture supports the creation of components that are interchangeable and reusable—in other words, plug and play.

Principle 1
Don't reinvent the wheel.

Principle 2
You won't do better than what's already been done.

Principle 3
Your customers don't know what they want.

Principle 4
Get something working as soon as possible.

Principle 5
Use sound software engineering practices.

Principle 6
Don't trust the client applications.

Principle 7
Plan to make changes.

Principle 8
You can't predict the future.

Principle 9
Don't tie your services into knots.

Principle 10
Build early, build often!

Principle 11
"What middleware?" should be your greatest compliment.

Principle 12
Expose the invisible.

Principle 13
Log everything.

Principle 14
Know the data.

Principle 15
Know when it will break.

Principle 16
Don't fail due to unexpected success.

The Martian Principles

PRINCIPLE

1

*Don't reinvent
the wheel.*

Now that's a good bit of advice, isn't it? Few would disagree with it, and yet we can easily fall into the trap of disregarding this fundamental principle. Here are a few common reasons:

- **We're just doing a small, simple system.** The assumption is that it isn't worth the effort or the cost to build a "real" enterprise system. If you really are just creating something trivial, then sure, do whatever works. But what starts out small and simple often grows into something more complex that must handle greater demands. If your system grows by tacking functionality onto an architecture that was meant for something far simpler, it will fail.

- **Our problem is unique.** Are you sure that your problem is different from anything anyone has ever solved before? Do you really believe that you need to invent a completely original solution? If so, that's beyond the scope of this book. Good luck!

- **We do not have time to do research.** So, you are in a big hurry, and you do not want to spend the time to find out what others have already done. But you do have time to charge off and develop something new, and then test it, and perhaps do it over again because the first attempt didn't work, and then test again, and develop again. Does this make any sense?

- **We want to invent something new.** This book is about building successful enterprise systems that will solve the problems in your domain. If your goal is to become rich and famous by devising new standards and inventing new infrastructure software, then you do not want to read this book. But I'll promise to read yours after you have become famous.

Someone Else Has Already Solved Your Problem

It is most likely that substantial portions of your problem have already been solved by others. Take advantage of their experience by reading their articles or using shareware they have contributed. Hire them if you can.

This is not to say that someone else's solution will always work for you. Every problem is different in some way, and no solution fits all. Identify what is unique about your problem and isolate those portions. Define these unique portions so that they are as small as possible. Then it will be worth your while to make the rest of your problem fit one or more of the previous solutions so that you can concentrate on your small, unique portion.

Understand What Your Added Value Is

You need to partition your problem into the portions that are unique to your domain and everything else. Your solutions to the unique portions of your problem represent your *added value*.

The added value of your enterprise system is what solves the particular problems of your domain. Everything else is mostly infrastructure, such as network protocols, security, scalability, and the like. Doing the added value right will make your system successful. Therefore, it makes sense to spend the larger amount of your time identifying, understanding, and creating your added value, and far less time on infrastructure code that others have already written.

Use Commercial Software Whenever Practicable

Commercial software packages are great at providing generic solutions to generic problems. You can configure most packages to solve a range of problems.

Use commercial software to build the nonunique portions of your system. Often this is your system's infrastructure. For example, a commercial application server can take care of network access, security, scalability, reliability, and so on. It is not worth your time, effort, and expense to build infrastructure and support code—good software vendors have already tested and validated their solutions, especially if their packages have been around for a while and have long lists of satisfied customers.

MISSION NOTES

Make vs. buy? That was an important question for the CIP middleware. Should we attempt to make a custom middleware infrastructure, or should we buy a commercially available application server?

We decided to purchase licenses for the WebLogic application server from BEA Systems to form the basis of CIP's middleware infrastructure. Our added value consists of the services we needed to develop to support the Mars rover mission, and these services run within WebLogic. Our task was not to invent and implement new middleware infrastructure standards. After all, the users benefit from the mission-related services that CIP provides, and the middleware just has to remain invisible but reliable. (I'll have more to say later about invisible middleware.)

Be wary of the trap of thinking you cannot afford a commercial solution. Carefully weigh the cost of purchasing software (and its support and maintenance) versus the cost of recreating it, especially if doing so takes resources away from working on your added value. Keep in mind that not getting the infrastructure right is a good guarantee that your enterprise system will fail—and failure can be very costly indeed.

You won't do better than what's already been done.

This principle is an adjunct to not reinventing the wheel. Really, unless you are a programming genius—I'll admit I'm not if you will admit you are not either—you are not going to do better than what has already been proven by industry to work. After all, companies need to make profits, and they will not if the software packages they use do not work. You will not see too many companies using faulty software, at least not for very long.

Adhere to Industry Standards and Best Practices

The key message behind this principle is that you should adhere to industry standards. Good standards organizations consist of representatives from many companies from a spectrum of industries, and they spend much time (often too much time) debating and working out issues in the open. They solicit and evaluate input from the public at large.

Standards do not get widespread adoption by industry unless they are practical. You had better have a very strong reason to develop nonstandard software. Your excuse may be expediency, but you will pay a heavy penalty down the road. Other software components may not work with your nonstandard components. You will need to spend time and money to train your developers to use your proprietary techniques. You may have a hard time hiring good developers.

Industry "best practices" are similar to industry standards. They are ways to do things—coding techniques, design methodologies, how to organize and build your code, and the like—that represent good experiences that other developers have collected over time across many projects. These are usually written up as articles in the various trade rags or on the Web, or after a while, they may be collected in books. Profit from the experiences of others!

MISSION NOTES

When I joined the CIP project, the mission was about a year from launching the first rover towards Mars, and 20 months from software code freeze. It was absolutely critical that we designed and developed the middleware infrastructure as quickly as possible and that it worked reliably to support the rest of the project. (The term "product launch window" takes on additional meanings at NASA!) The middleware absolutely could not be the bottleneck, and in fact, it sometimes had to take the lead position to pull the rest of the project forward.

Those were all strong arguments in favor of adhering to industry standards and best practices of J2EE and web services.

You might not be able to apply industry best practices if your system is proprietary and nonstandard.

Seek User Groups, Chat Forums, Online Documentation, Books, and the Like

When you adhere to industry standards and best practices, you join a large club of architects and developers. Seek out your fellow club members. Join user groups. Participate in chat forums. Read the most current online documentation. Purchase highly rated books.

Unless you have gone off to the fringes to do things differently from everybody else, you will not be alone in cyberspace. Your fellow club members will be there to help you. They will share their tips with you, and in turn, you can tell them what you have learned on your projects.

MISSION NOTES

We selected WebLogic, a popular commercial application server from BEA Systems that had been around for several years and therefore had a large user community. Documentation from BEA and other sources is available on the Web. There also are public online forums where users post questions and receive answers from BEA and other users. These are extremely helpful. We also purchased technical support contracts that gave us 24 × 7 phone support.

Do Not Gum Up the Plumbing

The bottom line is that you want the foundation, the infrastructure, the *underlying plumbing* of your enterprise system, to be stable. A shaky, leaky foundation is a guarantee of failure. Standards and best practices address system infrastructure, and they have been vetted and validated by industry. Adhere to them. No excuses.

*Your customers
don't know what
they want.*

Wait a minute—what happened to "The customer is always right"? That may be true in the retail business, but when it comes to designing and developing enterprise software systems, you may encounter customers who are clueless. So, how can you build them a successful system if they do not know what they want?

Do Not Push Too Hard on the Requirements

Of course, you need to get requirements from your customers, the future users of your system. After all, you are building the system for them. But enterprise systems are complex. Your customers probably have some ideas about what they want but most likely not the details.

Requirements specifications are all about the details. Many IT shops spend months, if not longer, trying to pin down and analyze the specifications. In fact, they often tell their customers that they will not start designing their systems until the requirements specs are done. That is a bad strategy that puts the customers under a great deal of pressure to write them.

So, what happens? The customers will make things up! They will put unreasonable requirements into the spec, just to put *something* down. (They may not realize that what they are asking for is unreasonable, only that it sounds good.) After all, time is money, and they want you to start building their system. The result is that you may be stuck with trying to design and build a system to meet bogus requirements.

Do Rapid Prototyping and Lots of User Testing

Like art, most customers do not know what they want until they see it. So, it is important to show them working code as soon as possible. Start coding as soon as the customers have workable ideas about what they want. Therefore, rapid prototyping and user testing are crucial.

MISSION NOTES

The mission managers at NASA's Jet Propulsion Laboratory (JPL) gave the CIP project team high-level requirements. As described in the Introduction of this book, CIP had to fulfill several major mission needs, including user management (who are you and what are you allowed to do?), time management (the mission has to deal with multiple Earth and Mars time zones simultaneously, and it initially ran on Mars time), personnel and event scheduling (lots of things happen during each day, and mission personnel with different roles and responsibilities have to stay coordinated), and the ability to browse and download mission data and images securely over the Internet.

The CIP team developed client tools that it believed would meet these requirements and the middleware services to support the applications. Time constraints made rapid prototyping crucial, and there were many iterations between the mission managers and the CIP developers. By working together, we converged towards tools and applications that met the requirements in ways that no one could have predicted at the beginning of the design process.

Once you show your customers some working code, they will say things like, "Yes, that's what I want!" or "That's close, but can you make such and such changes?" or "No, that's not what I want at all." Even if you show them something that's totally wrong, you and the customers have learned something useful about what they do want.

By doing rapid prototyping and lots of user testing, both you and your customers will converge towards the "correct" requirements specifications. At the end of this process, not only will you have all the requirements but you will also have a nice body of code that implements them.

Customers Are the Best Testers

It should be clear by now that your customers, the future users of your enterprise system, are the best testers. Not only are they looking for the features that they want, but they are also using these features *their way*, not necessarily the way you have designed them to be used.

The corollary to this principle is that the software architects and developers are the worst testers. Sure, we must do unit testing of our modules. But when it comes to testing the overall system, we tend to exercise the features the way we think they ought to be used. Only your future users know how they will really use the system. So, make sure there will be lots of user testing, and take really good notes during the tests.

MISSION NOTES

Before the rovers landed on Mars, JPL ran a series of Operational Readiness Tests (ORTs). Each ORT was a realistic simulation of mission operations. Fully functional, but Earth-based, rovers operated in a large "sandbox" that resembled the Martian surface inside a nearby warehouse. Mission personnel controlled these rovers remotely as if the rovers were on Mars, and they used all the supporting software as they would during the actual mission.

The CIP designers, along with the designers of the other software applications, participated in the ORTs as observers and gained invaluable feedback. We learned how our software would be used, which features worked and which didn't, and what improvements we needed to make.

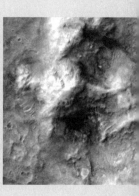

Get something working as soon as possible.

Once you have designed your enterprise software system, developing it will be a daunting task. It looks *so* complicated. Yikes! Where do you start?

There are several development approaches. A common one is to have several development teams working independently to develop the separate components of your system, and then try to put the components together into a working system. This is a dangerous approach. Often, the teams will spend longer than planned working in isolation on their components, and then it will be hard to get the components to work together. This integration may not happen until fairly late in the development cycle, and that violates the principle of doing rapid prototyping. Of course, you run the real risk that the components will not come together before the final deadline, in which case your enterprise project has failed.

Getting something working as soon as possible is one of the most important principles for ensuring success, especially for the most complex enterprise systems.

The First End-to-End Thread Is Critical

So, if you need to get something working as soon as possible, what should that *something* be?

The situation is analogous to building a bridge across a wide river. The first step is to get a strong rope across the river. That is a good first step because now you have something going across the river, and we can agree that you have made real progress towards building a bridge across the river. Once you have the rope, you can haul workers and materials across the river, and you can start to build the bridge framework.

At the onset of developing your enterprise system, look for a simple execution flow that goes from one end to the other end and back. In other words, have a client application make a simple request of the server, to which the server offers a simple response. This end-to-end thread of execution is your initial rope across the river. It does not matter if the initial client application is very simple, and the server code does not do much other than receive and acknowledge the client request.

The first end-to-end thread is critical for the ultimate success of your enterprise system because it establishes right at the very beginning that your infrastructure works and that your developers know how to use it. It is definitely worth spending time at the start of the development cycle to identify this first thread and to get it working. This is an effort for all the developers working together. Do not do anything else until this is done.

MISSION NOTES

We designed CIP to have a three-tiered service-oriented architecture (client, middleware, and data). Components in the middleware tier that implemented the services communicated with components in the other two tiers by using web services and synchronous and asynchronous messages. The system appeared dauntingly complex.

When we first began designing and developing the middleware, generating web services as interfaces to our components was a relatively new concept. We weren't sure that our development tools would be up to the task, or whether such a combination of these technologies would even work. The web services standards were new to many of the developers, so there was some apprehension.

Our first end-to-end thread was very straightforward: A small client application made a request to a web service and waited for the response. The web service had been deployed as the interface to a middleware component that made a simple query to a database in the data tier. The middleware component returned the fetched data to the client application as the web service response.

MISSION NOTES

Once we figured out how to build and deploy our first thread and get it to work, we learned how to use our development tools and how to integrate the components across all three tiers. This gave us the confidence and a template with which to develop the other services.

Working Code Builds Confidence

A journey begins with a single step, and that first step can be the hardest. Getting the first end-to-end thread working is your first step, and taking that step is a tremendous confidence builder for everybody: the architects, the developers, and the project managers.

The initial thread can serve as a model for the other components by demonstrating both how to write the code and how to integrate the code with the infrastructure. A working model makes rapid prototyping possible.

Always Build on Top of Working Code

You should always build on top of working code. The first end-to-end thread can be the root or foundation.

If you add new code on top of code that already works, you have a much better chance of getting the new code to work, too. If your system stops working, then that last piece of code you added must have broken it, so that is what you have to debug.

This development methodology greatly minimizes the chance that your final enterprise system, especially if it is complex, will have fundamental flaws or fail in mysterious ways.

MISSION NOTES

The CIP project was very strict about developers being responsible for checking into our source control system only code that had been tested and shown to work. We wrote many small test programs for doing regression testing to ensure that code that used to work still worked after we made changes elsewhere. Having a component-based, service-oriented architecture made it possible to partition the project into independent modules, each of which we could develop incrementally.

A good place to start, especially if you are having trouble getting even your initial thread to work, is one of the sample programs that often come with a commercial application server or a development tool. If even the simplest sample program does not work, then you may have a configuration problem that you must fix with the help of technical support from your software vendor.

PRINCIPLE

5

Use sound software engineering practices.

Who would not want to use sound software engineering practices? You would be surprised. Many architects and developers treat an enterprise system as if it was just another application to write, albeit a large one. However, an enterprise system presents many additional complexities, such as having components distributed over many machines but still (hopefully) cooperating with each other. Good software engineering is critical for success.

Use a Component-Based Architecture

Speaking of components, be sure to base your enterprise architecture on software components. Follow industry standards and best practices for designing the components.

Components force you to modularize your code. Components with well-defined interfaces can plug and play into the enterprise infrastructure. Each interface represents a contract between the supplier (the programmer who writes the component code)

MISSION NOTES

Developing component-based architectures for the CIP project was a natural consequence of using the Java Foundation Classes (Swing) in the client tier and Enterprise JavaBeans (EJBs) in the middleware tier. Both are heavily based on components.

A component-based architecture made it possible for the client tier to migrate from platform to platform. The CIP client application started out as Java applets and then we converted it relatively easily to a standalone desktop application. We were also able to take individual client components and plug them into a separate software framework that supported large touch-screen plasma displays.

and the consumer (the programmer of the code that uses the component). Once you have agreed to this contract, you can work separately with confidence that your code will ultimately be able to work together.

Several suppliers can provide components that perform different functions but share the same interface, and the consumer will be able to use any of them. A component can also have multiple consumers, which is another way of saying that component-based architectures encourage software reuse.

Use Design Patterns

During the past 50 years, software development methodologies have evolved to confront the rapidly increasing complexities of our systems.

In the beginning, programmers used low-level machine and assembly languages. Needless to say, few would want to develop an enterprise system that way today. High-level third-generation languages were major improvements—many applications were written in FORTRAN and COBOL, and much systems code was written in C. Soon there were debates over the safety of GO TO statements, and these debates led to the development of structured programming. After programmers got used to using the structured control constructs, along came object-oriented programming (OOP) to bundle code with the data. But even OOP wasn't enough. Often, poorly designed object hierarchies added complexities of their own.

Design patterns evolved partly from attempts to deal with the complications introduced by object-oriented programming. The patterns are based on object-oriented and structured programming techniques, and they represent models for how to design and develop code to solve a set of commonly occurring, generic problems. There are now a few dozen well-known patterns, and there are even sets of specialized patterns, such as those for developing enterprise systems. Well-trained software developers learn to recognize when to apply the appropriate patterns.

Design patterns represent some of the current best practices of the software development industry. They have been tested and shown to work when correctly applied. There are many books about design patterns, containing numerous examples written in various programming languages. Because these patterns have names, they facilitate communication about software design. For example, if you say that you are using the façade pattern, anyone who has studied design patterns will understand how you are solving a particular coding problem.

When structured programming became accepted, programmers didn't just avoid GO TO statements, but they also learned to design in a top-down manner, to decompose their programs into modules, and to express their algorithms only in terms of the structured constructs. Object-oriented programming was another major paradigm shift. It represented software design at a higher level—programmers trained themselves to think of their programs as composed of objects that were data combined with the algorithms that operated on the data, and about how these objects came into existence, communicated with each other, and died during the lifetime of the program.

Design patterns promise yet another paradigm shift and take you to an even higher level of thinking. Software architects and programmers will learn to recognize a set of patterns in the behavior of their software systems. Just as you learned to use only the structured programming constructs, you will learn to design and code to incorporate proven design patterns.

Structured programming and object-oriented programming were not silver bullets for dealing with software complexity, and neither are design patterns. But design patterns are powerful tools, and you should learn to use them correctly.

MISSION NOTES

Most of us probably weren't constantly thinking about design patterns on the CIP project. But we ended up using many of the common patterns (such as façade and delegation) implicitly, because Swing and EJBs are designed to use them. A strong argument for following industry standards and best practices is that they support the use of design patterns.

Get All the Development Team Members to Agree

Managing programmers has been compared to herding cats. Components, design patterns, or whatever software engineering practices will not help much if there is not agreement among the development team members to use them.

Here is where the system architect or the project manager must exercise strong leadership to get all the team members to agree on a set of practices to follow for the project. Be very wary of the (often self-designated) "superprogrammers" on the team who believe they should be allowed to design and code as they themselves see fit. Such individuals can be highly disruptive and harmful to overall team cohesion and morale.

MISSION NOTES

Fortunately, all the CIP project team members recognized the importance of good software engineering practices and the need for consensus. Of course, we had our occasional disagreements about which particular practices to follow or how best to implement them, but we always made sure to resolve them through meetings.

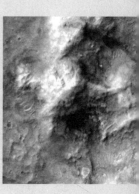

Don't trust the client applications.

Yes, it is quite harsh to say that you do not trust the client applications. After all, the client applications trust the middleware to provide them with reliable services. But a server failure caused by a single misbehaving client can adversely affect all the other client applications. Therefore, it pays for the middleware architect to be extra cautious about the client applications.

Be Very Paranoid— They *Are* Out to Get You

"Be very paranoid" is simply another way of saying, "Practice strong defensive programming."

As the middleware designer, you must recognize the simple fact that you often have no control over the users and their client applications. They may attack your middleware. There may very well be a few truly malicious users lurking out there, but let's assume that most attacks are not intentional.

Why do unintentional attacks occur? Most likely, the original design contracts between the client tier designers and the middleware designers weren't specific enough to cover all the pathological "corner cases," and so troublesome loopholes slip through undetected during development. For example, a problem not caught early in the development cycle could allow a client application to send a dangerous request to the middleware, and then a middleware service gets into trouble attempting to fulfill the request. In this example, the client application actually allows the user to attack the middleware. This can happen either when the user is first learning how to use the application or when the user is already familiar with the application and is experimenting with untried features.

In any case, if you are the middleware designer, you must carefully examine each and every request your code will service.

MISSION NOTES

CIP client applications do not directly access the databases in the data tier. Instead, the middleware provides a set of services that make calls to the database servers. A service request from a client application contains parameter values that the middleware service uses to formulate the proper database queries.

A CIP client tool offers several search features where a user enters search criteria that the tool submits as the request parameter values. The tool allows the user to specify wildcards to indicate "any value" as a parameter. What we failed to anticipate was what happens if a user enters wildcards into all the search fields. The middleware can end up fetching thousands, if not tens of thousands, of records from the database, far more than the network can transmit in a reasonable amount of time and certainly more than the client application can handle. Of course, this problem becomes progressively worse as the database grows larger. These bad queries tie up system resources unnecessarily.

A good defense would be for the middleware service to put a limit on the number of records that it fetches for any database query.

Ask yourself, "What can possibly go wrong with this request?" and put in adequate defenses.

If You Do Not Break It, They Will

How do you practice defensive programming? Two words: *imagination* and *testing*. You need to imagine what can possibly go wrong and design proper defenses. Then you must do lots of testing, during which you attempt to break through your defenses. I discussed user testing earlier, and I will cover stress testing later.

The bottom line is that if during the design and development phase, you do not find all the ways the users and their client applications can break the middleware, then surely they will while your system is in operation.

MISSION NOTES

Despite the few slipups such as the wildcard search criteria, the CIP client and middleware developers did work closely to prevent problems. But the real test for the middleware was presented by client applications that came onboard shortly before CIP became operational to take advantage of the middleware services.

These new client applications were not written by the CIP team, and one of them was not even written in Java. Because the middleware provided language-independent web services, it also supported a C++ client application. We had very little control over how they were written. Fortunately, we were able to accommodate the new applications safely.

PRINCIPLE

7

Plan to make changes.

Having a successful enterprise system at the moment you are ready to deploy it is not good enough. Were you able to incorporate those new last-minute requirements? If so, consider yourself lucky. But that's only the beginning. What about changes in the requirements after you have deployed the system, when it is already operational?

A successful enterprise system isn't one that's simply "right" at first deployment. A successful system must also expect and plan for future changes.

Do Not Hard-Code Values

Virtually all programs have values that they use internally. In an enterprise system, these values are embedded within each of the services provided by the middleware, and they also exist in the client programs. The values are parameters that affect the behavior of the services and programs.

Parameter values are not always passed in as program arguments or request parameters, but often they are hard-coded constants or literals within the source statements. They may be initial values, minimums and maximums of ranges, fixed indexes into tables or lists, or any constant value used in a computation.

The problem with hard-coded values is that they are hard to change once the system is deployed and operational. To make any change, you have to edit the source code, then recompile, retest, and redeploy it. That may not be straightforward in some operational environments, especially if you need to deal with a strict change review board.

Use External Editable Parameter Files

A winning strategy for developing successful enterprise systems is to identify these parameter values. Then instead of hard-coding them, supply the values at runtime.

MISSION NOTES

CIP uses Java properties files for its middleware services. In its initialization code, each middleware service reads its properties file. If we change any parameter values, every subsequent new instance of the service will get the new values.

An excellent way to do this is to employ parameter files. These files contain the parameter values in the form of keyword-value pairs. Each pair consists of the name of the parameter (such as ENDING_YEAR) and its value. At runtime, client programs and the middleware services read their parameter files to obtain the parameter values.

Parameter files are text files that are external to the software code. Therefore, you can edit the values without changing the code, so there are no recompilations and redeployments. It is a much safer procedure, and less testing and reviewing will be necessary.

Implement a "Read Parameters" Method

Have each middleware service implement a remote "read parameters" method. After editing a service's parameter file, you can invoke the method as a service request to tell a currently running instance of the service to read the file immediately and thus dynamically reconfigure itself. Of course, new instances of the service will read the changed parameter values upon initialization.

MISSION NOTES

We didn't do this with the CIP middleware services, because it is so easy to "hot-redeploy" a service, even when it is running, to force it to reinitialize and reread its properties file.

Maintain Client Parameter Files Centrally on the Server

Client programs also should use parameter files. But how do you manage these files? If the client programs are standalone desktop applications, then each user has a copy of the program and its parameter file on his or her local computer. If you need to change a parameter value, how do you update all the distributed copies?

Keep a master copy of the client program parameter file on the middleware server. Whenever a user starts the client application, the program makes a middleware service request to download a copy of the client parameter file, which the program can then read to get the latest parameter values.

Thus, you manage client parameter values centrally on the server. Whenever you make a change to a client parameter value, the very next user who starts the client application will get the new value.

MISSION NOTES

The CIP client application uses this technique of downloading its properties file from the middleware during initialization. It saves us from needing to provide client code upgrades to our users, which can have serious complications with users who aren't able or do not know how to install new software.

Identify the Parameter Values

It can be tricky to identify which values in your software are parameters. There are no simple rules, and you may just have to use your experience and intuition. You probably do not want to put every value in a parameter file, because that may hurt performance.

MISSION NOTES

In a complex enterprise system, you will not always get it right. We didn't with CIP. Who could have known that the rover mission would still be going after two years? The rovers were each designed to last 90 days, so they were to operate on Mars during the early months of 2004. One of the CIP client tools has a drop-down menu containing the years 2003, 2004, and 2005 covering the years that CIP would be used, including the flight time (2003), the time on the Martian surface (2004), and what we developers thought at the time was an extra year (2005) for good measure. Recently, we were asked to add the years 2006 and 2007. Unfortunately, we had hard-coded the menu items. Oops!

One of the Martian principles I describe later deals with unexpected success, such as your system being used far longer than you expected.

PRINCIPLE

8

You can't predict the future.

This principle is a follow-up to the previous one about planning for changes. Crystal balls are always in short supply, and the vision they provide of the future is usually murky at best. Since you cannot predict the future, you must design your enterprise system to adapt to whatever may come. There are ways to do this beyond using runtime parameter files.

Make Each Service Dynamically Reconfigurable

Dynamic reconfiguration refers to the ability for a deployed middleware service to change the way it operates, without first shutting down the service, or, in the worst case, shutting down the middleware server itself along with all the services.

The previous principle mentioned an important way to accomplish this, namely, parameter files that the services read upon instantiation or upon receiving a "read parameters" request.

The key idea is to keep each service running as long as possible so that client applications do not experience interruptions. If a service becomes unavailable, users will see a loss of functionality in the system and consider it downtime. They will not care if it is due to maintenance or a server problem.

Create Field-Replaceable, Plug-and-Play Services

Parameter files and dynamic reconfiguration means that you have designed alternate execution paths in the middleware services. This is practical if you can predict at design time what all the possible useful paths are.

But, of course, unexpected things can come up after you have deployed the services and your enterprise system is already operational. To handle such cases, you must design your middleware services to be plug and play and replaceable "out in the field."

Being plug and play is possible if your services adhere to standard interfaces. You can swap out a middleware service and "plug in" a replacement, and the new service will be able to "play" in place of the old one. The term "field-replaceable" comes from the hardware side, where a vendor's customer engineer can go out to a customer's site to replace a hardware component, with no need to shut down the computer system and send it back to the manufacturer. The situation is similar with software—you should be able to replace a middleware service without shutting down the customer's entire middleware.

MISSION NOTES

We designed and implemented each of CIP's middleware services using Enterprise JavaBeans, which guaranteed that each service adhered to the standards defined for EJBs. Thus, all our services were plug and play.

To replace a middleware service, we first upload the new code to the middleware server's file system. We then issue a remote command to the WebLogic application server to redeploy the service, which causes the new code to replace the old service code. This operation takes only a second or two, so most users do not notice any interruptions.

We used this capability during development. After our enterprise system became operational, it has not been necessary for us to replace a middleware service. So far, they have all been sufficiently reconfigurable via their parameter files.

Hot Redeployment Allows Reconfiguring without Rebooting

"Hot redeployment" is a feature of the middleware server that allows you to replace a running middleware service with a new one without first bringing down the server. When a service is about to be redeployed, the server must allow currently running instances of the service to complete fulfilling their requests and temporarily block new requests for that service. Once the last instance is done, the server swaps out the code and replaces it with the new code, and the service requests are unblocked. Again, the key idea is to keep the middleware running without interruption.

MISSION NOTES

The WebLogic application server handles all hot redeployments. This is an important reliability feature for the CIP middleware although, as mentioned above, we have not needed to use it so far.

We are also able to shut down individual services if necessary. For example, we needed to perform some maintenance work on several database tables in the CIP data tier. We shut down the middleware services that accessed those tables, and then restarted them when the maintenance work was done. Even though our users were not able to access those services (we had warned them ahead of time), they were still able to use the other services.

We have managed to keep the middleware server running continuously without interruption for months at a time. We have brought it down completely only when the mission needed to physically move our servers, or to do network maintenance.

Make Each Service Loosely Coupled

Having hot-redeployable middleware services is not useful if subsequently the client applications cannot use the replacement service. Therefore, it is crucial to design each service to be "loosely coupled."

A loosely coupled service maintains a fixed interface between the service provider and the service client. That enables the middleware to change the implementation of the service (such as after a hot redeployment) without requiring changes to the client application. The client applications and their users should not even have to know that a service implementation changed. The applications continue to make service requests and receive responses as before.

Take a Peek into the Future

You may not be able to predict the future, but it does not hurt to take some "what if" peeks into the future.

What if your system ends up with more users than you were originally told the system would have? What if the database grows larger than originally specified? These are potential occurrences in the future, and you should test the system's behavior by simulating these types of situations.

MISSION NOTES

In CIP, the interfaces between the client applications and the middleware were web services. Web services maintained the loose coupling, especially since the web services standard is language- and platform-independent.

Another simple check is to set the system clock of the middleware server or a client machine ahead a year or two. Does everything still work?

MISSION NOTES

Some of the CIP database tables did indeed grow much larger than we anticipated—the mission itself has lasted much longer than the originally specified 90 days, and the rovers continue to send down data. Fortunately, as mentioned earlier, we were able to shut down temporarily the middleware services that accessed those tables while we reindexed the tables to improve performance.

Early in the mission, we dodged a bullet that could have had CIP shut down mysteriously until we figured out the cause. One of our users complained that he could not log in. After several hours of investigation, we noticed that his workstation's clock was accidentally set ahead one month. That didn't explain why he couldn't log in, until we discovered that our middleware server license was going to expire in a few days! We had installed a nonexpiring license, but we had misconfigured it. The user could not log in because his workstation was already in the time after the license expiration.

We would have caught this problem earlier, before we deployed our software, had we tried setting our system clocks ahead a year to ensure that everything still worked.

Don't tie your services into knots.

The previous principle stressed designing loosely coupled services, where agreed-upon interfaces keep the client applications unaware of how you implemented the middleware services. This principle addresses how the services should relate to each other in the middleware server.

Keep Your Services Independent of Each Other

Be careful with interdependencies among your middleware services. Recall from the earlier principles that you want to be able to reconfigure services dynamically or do hot redeployment. This will be more difficult, or even impossible, if you have tied your services into knots with a web of interdependencies. Minimize the number of interdependencies as much as possible.

One of the major benefits of a component-based architecture is code reuse. A component designed for one middleware service might be used in another service. Be sure that shared components among the services do not introduce unwanted interdependencies. If you modify a shared component, you may be forced to redeploy each service that uses that component.

If you discover a component that performs several unrelated functions for different services, you should split it into several components.

Services Should Treat Other Services As Equals

If middleware Service A needs some data provided by middleware Service B, then Service A should make a request of Service B and get a response. As middleware designers and

MISSION NOTES

The CIP middleware services are mostly separate from each other. Only one of the services requires data from another one. An EJB of the first service sends a remote request to an EJB of the second service.

developers, do not make use of "insider knowledge" that services A and B reside on the same middleware server and then use a more efficient backdoor method for A to get data from B. Having middleware services calling each other on the server using a backdoor blurs the separation among the services and adds complexity if there are now multiple ways for a service to receive requests.

You may discover later that to improve performance, you need to distribute the middleware services among multiple servers. If Service A makes normal requests of Service B, then it will be much easier to move Service B to another server.

PRINCIPLE
10

Build early,
build often!

Asure way to disaster is to wait until the last minute to put your enterprise system together. If you do so, you will discover some very unpleasant truths, such as components that do not work well together, or components that will not come together at all.

You must start doing system builds very early during the development cycle. Your very first build can be the one for the initial end-to-end thread that you get working. Thereafter, you should do builds often, certainly after adding any significant new code.

Some projects adopt a "build as needed" policy, which can work well for small project teams, as long as the builds do not happen too far apart. Other projects do nightly builds so that the development team can always expect a fresh system each morning that incorporates all of the previous day's changes.

The Major Challenge Is Not Code Development but Code Integration

Ask architects, developers, or project managers what is hard about developing enterprise systems, and many will tell you that it is the programming.

In most cases, that is wrong. Most enterprise systems are sufficiently complex that the major challenge is not code *development*, but code *integration*. Code integration is about putting all the pieces together into the working whole. In other words, it is about doing successful system builds.

When you follow industry standards and use a commercially available application server, *how* to write your code has already been defined for you. Your client-side and your middleware code must use the application programming interfaces (APIs) that have been defined for the infrastructure. So, you do not have much leeway regarding how your components fit into the enterprise infrastructure.

But having the components call the standard APIs and fit into the infrastructure will not guarantee that the components will actually work well together. Components written by different programmers may pass their individual unit tests but then fail when they have to interact with other components. Client components may invoke the services of the remote server components in ways that the middleware programmers didn't expect, or the middleware components may return results to the client components in a manner that surprises the client application developers.

The primary cause of code integration problems is miscommunication among the members of the development team, or insufficient communication. One developer forgets to tell another

MISSION NOTES

There were about 12 developers on the CIP project. Although we were all located on the same NASA campus, we were spread throughout one building, and some worked in another building.

We realized that communication was important. There were many face-to-face conversations among the developers, many e-mail messages and phone calls, and regular team meetings. During the most intensive times, the entire team met twice weekly. Smaller groups, such as the client application developers, had separate meetings. The middleware group was small (three of us), and we usually met informally on an as-needed basis.

As the architect and lead on the middleware, it was very important for me to stay in constant communication with my counterparts in the client and the data tiers.

Code integration was challenging. Although we all programmed all the nondatabase code in Java, each group used different tools and methodologies to develop and deploy code.

developer about the change in behavior of a component, or they make wrong or obsolete assumptions about each other's work.

Open communication among the project team members and frequent system builds are the solutions to code integration problems.

Use a Source Code Repository

You must have a central code repository that does version management and revision control. If you cannot locate source files that went into builds, or if you lose track of which versions of the files were integrated into different builds, then your project is certain to fall into chaos and fail.

A developer who wants to modify a source file needs to "check out" the file from the code repository and then do a "check-in" when the modification is done. The repository needs to handle cases where two developers want to modify the same file at the same time. Either the repository should disallow this—the first developer who checks out a file locks out others from checking out the same file—or the repository must have a way to reconcile and merge changes made simultaneously by multiple developers.

An important rule is that any code checked into the repository must have been unit tested. In other words, no developer should ever check in any code that will not compile or is known to work incorrectly.

MISSION NOTES

The CIP project team used the CVS source code repository. We checked in not only the source code but also scripts and configuration files.

Maintain a Separate Environment in Which to Build and Deploy

Different project team members may have their own prefer-ences regarding tools and methodologies for developing and deploying their code. Some projects may be strict about having a common set of tools. But even then, tools appropriate for developing client applications may not be appropriate for mid-dleware developers. Database developers usually have a dif-ferent set of tools altogether.

To ensure successful system builds, a project needs to follow a few basic ground rules.

System builds should always be done with the latest ver-sions of the code files taken from the source code repository. If you allow developers to insert their private copies of code files into the build, you will soon lose track of which versions of files are in the build and where they came from. This situation will lead very soon to unreliable and unreproducible builds.

Even though tools such as integrated development environ-ments (IDEs) are extremely useful for code development, system builds should not rely upon them. IDEs may have their own ver-sions of libraries, and you will run the risk of losing track of which libraries you used. Other development tools may have idiosyncrasies that you want to avoid. You certainly do not want to rely on always having the right versions of these tools around even after development is complete.

Therefore, system builds should occur in a separate and clean environment, preferably on a hardware server that is iso-lated from the developers' workstations. After extracting the latest versions of the source files from the repository, use the most basic tools to build and deploy the system. This often means command-line-based tools that you can incorporate into command scripts.

When you do your systems builds and deployments using scripts in a separate environment without any dependencies on the developers' tools, you are assured that you can always reproduce the system. This will be true even after you have moved the system builds and deployments to a different location, such as your production servers.

MISSION NOTES

All our system builds occurred on a server that was not also someone's development workstation. Even though different developers had their favorite editors and development tools, the builds and deployments were all done by basic command-line tools that we scripted using ANT.

The ANT scripts extracted the latest sources from CVS, compiled them with the *javac* command, invoked any necessary WebLogic development utilities, and then deployed the system to our internal application server for testing.

We used these ANT scripts to perform regular system builds. Developers often used the same scripts to build and deploy personal copies of the system to facilitate unit testing. Using the same scripts helped to ensure that code, after it had been checked into the repository, would not break the master build. In the end, we used the same scripts to do the final build and deployment.

"What middleware?" should be your greatest compliment.

One day, when I was meeting with a CIP user, I happened to mention CIP's middleware. His reply was, "What middleware? I just log in with my laptop, request the image file I want, and after a few seconds, the image just shows up on my screen. What is this 'middleware' you claim I'm talking to?"

I was a bit taken aback by this user's remarks, as I was quite proud of the CIP middleware. But after some reflection, I realized that I had actually been paid a great compliment.

The Middleware Should Be Invisible to Users

What is the purpose of an enterprise system's middleware? It has many roles. It receives service requests from client applications and routes these requests to the appropriate service provider component, and then it transmits the service response back to the client application. It controls the service providers' access to the data sources. It provides security features, such as user accounts, access privileges, and encrypted data transfers. By managing all of its components that provide services, the middleware ensures a high level of reliability, availability, and scalability.

But the bottom line is that the middleware exists to support the client applications. Simply stated, you want the middleware to make the client applications look good.

Middleware that does its job well should be invisible to the end users. If they notice it is there, even if they are not sure what it is, then something has gone seriously wrong with the enterprise system.

Being a middleware architect or developer is not on the path to fame and glory, at least not with the end users. That would be reserved for the client application developers, whose work the users see directly, and the designers of the back-end data repositories, who make available all the data the users desire. If you are a middleware architect or developer, you will just have to learn to derive personal satisfaction from knowing that your efforts behind the curtain make the enterprise system work well.

Good Middleware Creates Ideal Virtual Worlds for the End Users

Middleware that is well designed and functioning properly creates virtual worlds for the end users.

Users should believe that the client applications *are* the entire enterprise system. A user should log in to a client application that appears to do everything by itself. The user should not be concerned with connecting to the network, talking to the middleware server, or accessing remote databases. It should appear that the client application knows how to provide all the desired services and magically make the data available.

Good middleware should create the illusion for each end user that he or she has exclusive access to the system's data and services. This means, of course, that the middleware must be reliable and scale well in response to heavy loads.

Enterprise systems that support user collaboration rely upon their middleware to create virtual communities. This entails middleware features such as messaging and shared data. Good middleware creates the illusion that the users can connect directly with each other.

To keep the middleware hidden from the users, they should never directly see warning or error messages generated by the middleware. Users should only see messages that are understandable to them and relevant to the operations of the client applications. Therefore, the application developers should write these messages. The middleware has the responsibility to provide sufficient status information for the applications to produce meaningful messages.

MISSION NOTES

As I related in my anecdote, CIP's end users generally are not aware of the middleware, nor do they have to think about connecting to remote servers.

Client applications that use CIP's middleware services are either "thick client" standalone desktop applications, or they are "thin client" browser-based applications. Most users realize they are going over the Internet, and so users can run CIP applications from anywhere they have valid Internet connections.

Expose
the invisible.

The previous principle emphasized the importance of keeping an enterprise system's middleware invisible to the end users. This principle is about exposing what is invisible, but to the system administrators who are monitoring the system.

Put Hooks in the Middleware

Middleware that is invisible to the end users should be very visible to its developers and, after the enterprise system has been deployed, to the system administrators who monitor the system.

Most commercial application servers include a "console" application that allows you to do housekeeping chores such as deploying new middleware services, tweaking parameter values, and monitoring performance. This console application is very useful and often crucial, but because it is supplied by the vendor of the application server, it tends to be oriented towards the operation of the server itself.

To monitor how your middleware services are behaving, you need to design hooks into the code to trap and expose key events and values that are pertinent to the operation of the services. You can log this information stream (the subject of the next principle), or you can accumulate and aggregate the data in a shared memory resource of the middleware. Depending on the service, this live operational data can provide you with anything from something as simple as the service is alive to a detailed blow-by-blow account of what the service is doing.

Of course, you need to consider the effect on performance of these code hooks. A good strategy is to have a high "sampling rate" while you are developing a service and then to throttle back when you are convinced the service is working as it should.

MISSION NOTES

Each CIP middleware service has a standard set of monitoring hooks. One hook traps the deployment or redeployment of the service. Other hooks trap service requests from the client applications.

The middleware developers put in other hooks that were relevant to the particular services they were developing. For example, the streamer service, which accesses and downloads files from the mission file server, has hooks that monitor the location and size of each file that it fetches.

Do Runtime, Real-Time Monitoring

Once you have all the monitoring hooks in place in the middleware services, you can develop an application that taps into the operational data streams and generates a real-time display.

You can design this monitoring application to be like any other client application that logs in and connects to the middleware. Then, you will be able to run the monitoring application anywhere you can run the other client applications.

The ability to do real-time monitoring of operational middleware services provides the middleware developers and, later, the system administrators much assurance that all is well with the services. This is especially important if reliability and high performance of the enterprise system are critical.

MISSION NOTES

We developed and deployed a CIP middleware service whose sole function is to respond to requests to access the operational data generated by the monitoring hooks.

Then we created a client application, the Middleware Monitor Utility. This utility makes periodic requests for the operational data, which it displays in real time using both text and graphics (see Figures 12-1, 12-2, and 12-3 for screen shots). This utility has proven to be extremely useful during the mission, since a quick glance at its display gives you a very good idea of how well the middleware is performing.

We also run a cron job on the middleware server that automatically takes snapshots of the same information every four hours and sends it by e-mail to a mailing list of people who need to keep tabs on the health of the CIP (see Figure 12-4).

Even now, two years into the mission, we continue to rely on the monitor utility and the cron job.

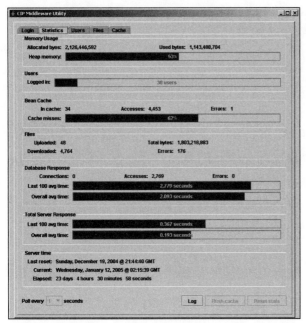

Figure 12-1: The CIP Middleware Monitor Utility's statistics tab, showing current middleware memory usage, the number of CIP users logged in, middleware cache usage and hit rate, the total number and sizes of files uploaded and downloaded, the number of database accesses and average response time (overall and over the last 100 accesses), the average middleware server response time (overall and over the last 100 accesses), and the current server time. At the time this screen shot was taken, the rover mission had already lasted three times longer than originally planned. The Middleware Monitor Utility indicated that the CIP database, which had grown very large, needed reindexing to improve its performance.

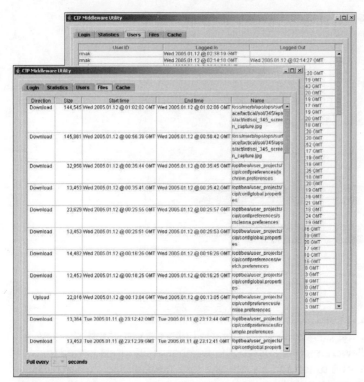

Figure 12-2: The Users tab and the Files tab of the CIP Middleware Monitor Utility. The Users tab shows the login and logout times of the CIP users. The Files tab shows statistics about the files that the streamer service has uploaded or downloaded: size, start time, end time, and path name.

Figure 12-3: The Cache tab of the CIP Middleware Monitor Utility shows the current contents of the middleware cache as expandable tree branches. Double-clicking on a tree leaf shows the actual data that was cached for a particular database query. The tab also shows the most recent load times of the databases.

```
Current time: Wednesday, October 19, 2005 @ 04:00:08 GMT
Up time: 138 days   1 hour   53 minutes   44 seconds

Heap memory allocated bytes: 2,126,446,592

Users logged in: 18
Cache accesses: 19,406   hit rate: 18%   errors: 0
Files uploaded: 281   downloaded: 22,376   total bytes:
7,757,897,827
Database accesses: 16,071   avg. response time: 0.069
sec.   errors: 0
Server avg. response time: 0.09 sec.

Last data loads:
    MER_A: Fri 2005.06.03 @ 02:10:22 GMT
    MER_B: Fri 2005.06.03 @ 02:10:22 GMT
    MER_T: Fri 2005.06.03 @ 02:10:22 GMT
    POISE: Wed 2005.10.19 @ 03:35:09 GMT
```

Figure 12-4: Some of the CIP middleware server statistics automatically e-mailed every four hours.

Log everything.

R eal-time monitoring, as described in the previous principle, is useful for letting you know what's happening *right
now*. On the other hand, logging gives you an "audit trail" and
a historical record.

You can use the same hooks that you put into the middleware
for monitoring to do logging. Of course, logging is not only useful in the middleware. Client applications and back-end data
utilities should also create logs.

Do Not Turn Off Logging in Your Production Code

There is a fable about a sailboat crew whose members all wore
their lifejackets while they were taking sailing lessons in the
harbor. But when they finally ventured out into the ocean, none
of them donned the jackets. Needless to say, all hands were lost
when the boat got into trouble and sank far from any help.

Logging is somewhat like that. During the development of a
client application or a middleware service, you might log prac-
tically everything, perhaps with simple "print" statements, to
help you debug your code. But you may be tempted to remove
or comment out the logging statements just before you deploy
the code to the production servers. However, of course, you
then run the risk of suffering the fate of the hapless sailboat
crew if your code ever crashes mysteriously.

A good logging package is important to have in place both
during development and when the code is operational.

Your logger should allow you to specify logging message
levels, preferably in an external parameter file. Message levels
could be, for example, *informational*, *debugging*, *warning*, and
error, in increasing order of severity. During development, you
can set the message level to *informational* or *debugging* to have
the logger output as many messages as you need to develop
your code. You can later increase the message level to *warning*

or *error* when your code is operational to decrease the number of messages.

Another important feature for a logging package is management of the log files. Preferably, each client application, middleware service, and back-end data utility should have its own log file. A good logger allows you to specify a maximum size for each log file, and as soon as the file reaches that maximum size, the logger automatically archives the file and immediately creates a new one. Some loggers may allow a log file to remain open all day and then archive it overnight and create a fresh file for the next day.

Do some experiments to see how logging affects performance. Remember that with enterprise systems, network latency is a key performance factor. You may discover that, relatively speaking, logging has less of an impact than you think.

MISSION NOTES

CIP uses the open-source Log4j package from the Apache Jakarta project. Each middleware service, client application, and back-end data utility keeps its own log.

The middleware services log at a low severity level, since we did discover that logging does not have a large impact on performance. At minimum, each service logs each request, and each log entry contains a timestamp, the ID of the user making the request, and the name of the method that the user's client application called to make the request. Most of the services logged other relevant information. See Figure 13-1 for sample log entries from the streamer service.

Logging was helpful during code development, of course, but it also proved invaluable during the first few weeks after CIP became operational. The logs enabled us to determine quickly the cause of any problems that occurred during those early days.

```
2004-12-20 20:23:33,435 INFO : mjane:
Streamer.putDataFile(/opt/bea/user_projects/cip/
conf/preferences/m.preferences)2004-12-20 20:23:33,439 DEBUG: Begin
upload of file '/opt/bea/user_projects/cip/conf/
preferences/sthompso.preferences'2004-12-20 20:23:39,140 DEBUG:
Completed upload of file '/opt/bea/user_projects/cip/conf/
preferences/sthompso.preferences': 35659 bytes
'/opt/bea/user_projects/cip/conf/global.properties': 13453 bytes
2004-12-20 20:28:57,516 INFO : jdoe: Streamer.getPreferences(user)
2004-12-20 20:29:29,721 INFO : jdoe: Streamer.getFileInfo()
2004-12-20 20:29:30,784 INFO : jdoe:
Streamer.getFileInfo(/oss/merb/ops/ops/surface/
tactical/sol)2004-12-21 19:17:43,320 INFO : jqpublic:
Streamer.getDataFile(/global/nfs2/merb/ops/ops/
surface/tactical/sol/120/opgs/edr/jpeg/1P138831013ETH2809P2845L2M1.JPG)2
004-12-21 19:17:43,324 DEBUG: Begin download of file
'/global/nfs2/merb/ops/ops/surface/
tactical/sol/120/opgs/edr/jpeg/1P138831013ETH2809P2845L2M1JPG'2004-12-21
19:17:44,584 DEBUG: Completed download of file
'/global/nfs2/merb/ops/ops/
surface/tactical/sol/120/opgs/edr/jpeg/1P138831013ETH2809P2845L2M1.JPG':
```

Figure 13-1: Sample log entries from the CIP streamer service. The log entry for each service request includes a timestamp, the user's name, the name of the request and its parameter value, the path name of the requested file, and the number of bytes uploaded or downloaded.

"Log Mining" Reveals Usage Patterns

In a heavily used enterprise system, it will not be long before you have many log files. These files are useful not only for solving problems.

You can write programs to analyze the log entries. By doing "log mining," you can glean useful information about the operation of your system that would otherwise be difficult to obtain, such as usage patterns. Knowing usage patterns enables you to tweak the system parameters to improve performance and otherwise provide a better user experience.

Plan ahead what you want to learn about your system's behavior from log mining, and you can design your log entries appropriately.

MISSION NOTES

CIP's middleware streamer service downloads requested files from the mission file server. By analyzing its log entries, we can generate graphs of the number of bytes downloaded over time. Thus, we can see how significant mission events (such as a rover making a discovery or taking an interesting photograph) affect data downloading by users (see Figure 13-2).

Log mining also shows us what data users are accessing from the back-end databases, and how they are doing it. This information enables us to optimize database performance.

Files and Bytes Downloaded

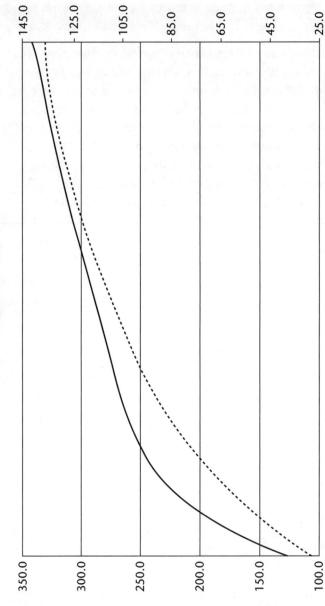

Figure 13-2: A graph of the cumulative number of files (solid curve) and bytes (dashed curve) downloaded by CIP during the mission. These plots were generated from values "mined" from the streamer service logs.

PRINCIPLE

14

Know the data.

Most enterprise systems are all about operations on data, including accessing, creating, transporting, converting, filtering, composing, displaying, and updating. Client applications provide interfaces that allow end users to initiate these and other operations.

It is not surprising, then, that in order to design and develop a successful enterprise system, you need to know the data.

Learn the Data Usage Patterns

What data do the end users want to access, and what will they do with the data? What operations will their client applications perform on the data?

These are some of the questions you need to answer before you can design the middleware services that will be the intermediary between the end users' client applications and the data sources. Not knowing the answers, or having incorrect answers, will cause you to design applications and services that do not do what the users want, or that perform poorly.

MISSION NOTES

The CIP development team had several key sources of information about data usage patterns. The mission requirements for CIP gave us initial ideas about what data users needed to access and what they were going to do with the data. During the many operational readiness tests at JPL, we observed users working with early versions of the applications, and we also met with the users and asked questions about what they would be doing during the mission. Finally, we analyzed the logs generated by the middleware services.

The data usage patterns tell you what data operations the users and their client applications want to perform, how they initiate the operations, how often they perform certain operations, and in what combinations.

Create Appropriate Application and Middleware Data Models

Application data models and middleware data models are the data structures that the client applications and their supporting middleware services, respectively, use to represent the data. The models represent how your software views the data, and you want the models to be optimal for the data usage patterns.

If you are the client application architect, you need to design a data model that is relevant to the problem domain of the application, and it must also make sense from each end user's point of view. The model should contain objects that the client applications can present to the users, and the users must understand and manipulate these objects.

The data model of the middleware services that support a client application may be very similar to the application data model. But if you are the middleware architect, you may need to view data more abstractly. Your middleware data model may be shared by several client applications, and you are also concerned with issues such as security, concurrency, transactions, and caching.

So, there may be data model transformations as data flows between the client applications and the middleware, such as during data marshaling and unmarshaling. The client application and middleware architects and developers must communicate well with each other and do rapid prototyping to ensure these transformations occur correctly and with good performance.

Middleware architects also need to pay attention to data usage patterns. You will want to know what types of data your services will handle most, so you can optimize the appropriate routines. If users ask for the same data repeatedly, you may want to cache the data in memory. Of course, if the data can be updated, then you will need to ensure that no cached data becomes stale.

MISSION NOTES

CIP uses web services for client applications to communicate with their middleware services, so the application data models are transformed during the conversions into and out of the eXtensible Markup Language (XML) data types used by the Simple Object Access Protocol (SOAP) and defined by the web services standard. The CIP application developers worked very closely with the middleware developers to ensure that such transformations happen with acceptable performance.

One of our few design failures involved data caching in the CIP middleware. While we were designing the metadata service, we believed that the metadata would be updated infrequently, and so we implemented a very simple caching scheme. After CIP became operational, we discovered that the metadata is actually updated very frequently, and the middleware had problems refreshing the cache at high rates. Fortunately, we designed the metadata service so that by a setting in its external parameter file, we could tell the service to turn off data caching. So now that service currently runs less efficiently than we wanted it to. The lesson we learned here: Do not try to do your own data caching. Use the caching software provided by the application server. If we were to redesign the CIP middleware, we would consider using the J2EE entity beans or packages such as Java Data Objects (JDO).

Map to Practical Physical Data Models

Physical data models represent how data is stored, such as in files or in databases.

When the middleware stores data, it maps middleware data models to the physical models. Conversely, when the middleware retrieves data, it maps physical data models to middleware data models. In both cases, data transformations occur.

The middleware architect must work closely with the back-end database and file system architects to ensure the application-level data models and the physical data models are well suited for each other. But the data architects also need to work closely with the client application architects, since the applications and the end users are the ultimate customers of the data.

Data modeling is a critical activity that involves the designers and developers throughout all tiers of an enterprise system.

Adapt to Third-Party and Legacy Data

You are very lucky indeed if you are able to design an entire enterprise system from scratch. But you may not have that luxury with the physical data models.

MISSION NOTES

CIP middleware services access data files in the mission file server, so we wrote adapters to read the mission file formats. Other middleware services access databases with legacy schemas. For those services, our adapters use database views that create virtual tables that map more easily to our middleware data models.

Physical data models tend to be the most inflexible. Your system may need to access data created by third parties over which you have no control. Your system may need to work with legacy data created long ago by other applications.

Instead of perverting your application and middleware data models, you should design the middleware services to incorporate software adapters to handle the third-party or legacy physical data models. Such adapters can perform any required data type conversions, semantic transformations (such as changing measurement units), or recombining data fields. The adapters will isolate your middleware services and client applications from any inappropriate attributes of the third-party or legacy data.

Know when it will break.

Your enterprise system is finally up and running, and you are close to deploying it. Is development done?

Do Lots of Stress Testing

Having all the client applications, middleware services, and back-end data utilities coded and integrated and working well together across all the tiers is a *major* accomplishment.

How did you determine that your enterprise system is really working? Did you create a user account for each of your developers and for each helpful volunteer you recruited from other departments? You might even have a QA department that provided a number of testers. Then did you ask everybody to log in, preferably many at the same time, and run the various client applications? Perhaps you even provided written up-to-date scripts for the testers to follow to make sure that they exercised all of the client application features.

This type of system check-out is important to ensure that your enterprise system is fully functional, that all the components do work together, and that the system is reliable. But should this be the "final" system check-out?

How many users will your system have? How many do you anticipate will be using the system at the same time? Unless you have at least that many people testing the system, you do not really know how reliable it is when it is under a heavy load.

Before you deploy the system, invest some time into doing stress testing. Unlike functionality testing that's best done by people to make sure that everything works, stress testing makes sure the system can handle heavy peak loads.

You probably will not be able to recruit enough volunteers to do stress testing manually. Instead, you will need to do it with automation by having a set of computers that simulate dozens, or perhaps hundreds, of end users running client applications.

There are commercial utilities that will do stress (or load) testing. You program the utilities using scripts that direct them to perform operations on your enterprise system and generate any desired load. If you can afford it, purchasing one of them is definitely the way to go.

A decent stress tester is not very hard to write. It is essentially a client application that spawns threads that represent users. Each thread simulates the behavior of a typical end user by logging into the system, performing some operations, and then logging out. You should run copies of the stress tester on various workstations on different parts of the network so that you do not overload any single workstation or any part of the network.

Each thread that simulates a user should choose from a list of operations. Add some randomness so that not every thread does the same things the same way in the same order. Stress testing is not necessarily functionality testing, so the stress tester does not have to exercise every possible operation. You want to see how the system performs under heavy load, which the stress tester can accomplish with just the most typical operations.

Of course, during stress testing is a very good time to run your middleware monitoring programs, and certainly examine the middleware service logs afterwards. The usage patterns may be artificial, but you should learn how the various system components interact under heavy load.

MISSION NOTES

The CIP middleware team wrote its own stress tester. It connected to the middleware like any other client program. It had a simple graphical user interface (GUI) that allowed us to specify the number of users to simulate, which operations to perform, and what should be the average "think time"—the amount of time to pause between operations by each simulated user. The stress tester randomized the order it performed the operations, and it varied the "intensity" of the operations, such as the sizes of files to download or the numbers of database records to fetch. A simple bar graph dynamically indicated the average response time of the middleware as experienced by the simulated users (see Figure 15-1).

During the last few weeks before we deployed CIP, we ran copies of our stress tester simultaneously on various developers' workstations. We learned how well the entire CIP system behaved under heavy load, from the client side through the middleware to the data tiers.

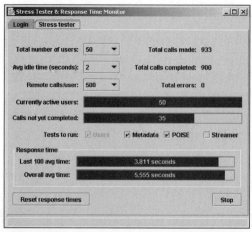

Figure 15-1: The client interface of the CIP Stress Tester utility. It doubles as a response time monitor by periodically sending a random request to the middleware server (at a much lower rate than during stress testing, of course).

If You Do Not Find Out What the Limits Are, Your Users Surely Will

Unless your enterprise system will never see heavy loads, manual functionality testing will not provide adequate stress testing. You must know how your system will handle the peak loads.

It almost goes without saying that if you do not find out what the limits of your system are, your users will after you have deployed the system and it is operational. During times of high usage (and high visibility), something will break, and your system will fail.

Before you deploy your system, run your stress testers to impose a load beyond what you would reasonably expect ever to happen in real life. Increase the stress until the system does break, and note what the breaking points are.

When your system is operational, monitor its performance with those breaking points in mind. You will know when you are approaching them in time to add more resources, such as more memory or servers, increased network capacity, or more storage space for the back-end databases.

If you have done adequate stress testing before deployment, you will have much greater confidence in the reliability and scalability of your enterprise system.

*Don't fail due to
unexpected success.*

Y̶ou may be so worried about unplanned failures that you may forget to consider unexpected success! Too much success can be stressful on an enterprise system, too.

Missions May Last Longer Than Expected

The preceding Martian principle was about stress testing and making sure that your enterprise system can withstand heavy peak loads. But another form of stress happens when your system remains operational beyond the time for which it was originally specified. What happens if the end users continue to use your system far longer than you expected?

Each day can be the proverbial straw that breaks the camel's back. One by one, tolerances that you built into your system are exceeded. Your data structures throughout the system become fragmented and polluted with uncollected garbage.

How can you mitigate this situation?

Some of the previous principles are very helpful. Do not hard-code any limit values, but instead, put them into parameter files so that you can adjust them if needed. You may need to do in-place hot redeployments of some middleware services in order to "reboot" them to a clean state.

After you are done stress testing for peak loads, do stress testing for longevity. Adjust your stress tester not to generate heavy loads but instead a moderate steady load. Then run several instances of it over a long period and observe the incremental effects on your enterprise system. See which tolerances are reached first.

It is always wonderful to deploy an enterprise system that performs well and meets all its requirements. But if the system's success causes it to be used longer than originally planned, you do not want that success eventually to cause a failure.

NOTES

...ded on Mars in January 2004 and were only
...days. As of December 2005, both are still
...face and sending back data and images.
...tinuously operational since December
...few interruptions. Since we followed these
...ciples while designing and developing the enter-
...stem, it has been holding up remarkably well. Like
the rovers, we're beginning to be concerned about hardware
failures as electronic and mechanical components of our
servers start to wear out.

Data Repositories May Grow Larger Than Planned

Often, when an enterprise system runs for an unexpectedly
long period, the back-end data repositories such as files and
databases may grow larger than planned. The consequence will
be slower performance. You may need to defragment the file
systems and move unused files to archives. You may need to
clean the databases of unused records and then reindex them.

Design your middleware services that access the data repositories to accommodate these and other performance-improving
operations. A simple way to achieve this is to make sure that
you can temporarily shut down only the affected services and
then restart them after the back-end operations are finished.

MISSION NOTES

After the rovers' 90-day mission had lasted about a year, some of the CIP functions began to have poor performance. Our back-end metadatabase had grown very large and contained many unused records.

We warned all the CIP end users that we needed to schedule some time for maintenance, and that certain client application functions would be unavailable temporarily. We shut down the metadata service while our database administrator purged the unused records and reindexed the tables, and then we restarted the service. Meanwhile, the other parts of CIP continued to run, and users who performed operations that didn't involve metadata were not affected.

Principle 17
Strong leadership drives a project to success.

Principle 18
Don't ignore people issues.

Principle 19
Software engineering is all about the *D*'s.

Principle 20
The formulas for success aren't complicated.

Project Management and Software Engineering

PRINCIPLE
17

Strong leadership drives a project to success.

A n enterprise system project, even if it has a good architect and skilled developers, will not simply "happen" to succeed. It needs to be driven to success by strong leadership.

Much has already been written about good leadership, but two salient qualities are (1) knowing where to lead the team, and (2) knowing how to convince the team members that they want to go there. Both the system architects and the project managers need to provide strong project leadership.

A Good Architect Must Also Be a Good Leader

In my personal experience as a software architect and from observing excellent software architects, I have learned that it is not just about design. If you create superb designs one after another but then you walk away from each one and allow someone else to implement it, will you still be considered a good architect?

To be a good architect, you must have good people skills. This may be challenging, since most technical people tend to have poor social skills. But a good architect must also be a leader, and leadership requires the ability to work with other people.

Good architects are the driving forces behind software development projects. As an architect, you determined the structure of the software and what components will go into it. Now it is your responsibility to lead the developers to implement your design.

Strong leadership is especially important if you are the middleware architect because, quite literally, you are right in the middle of all the development. You will need to work with the architects in the client and data tiers. You can exercise strong leadership and pull the entire project forward, or you can be the bottleneck that drags the whole project down. (I recommend the former!)

Any Architecture Is Only As Good As Its Implementation

Take a look at your house. What do you see? Do you see an architect's blueprint, or do you see walls, doors, windows, and a roof? Yes, it is great to have good architecture, but what you really appreciate about your house are those physical components. Good architecture for your house is worthless if it was sloppily built.

It may be unfair, but as an enterprise system architect whose architecture may have many implementations, you will be judged on the worst implementation. You may have to put in many years of hard work to attain a reputation for being a good architect. But you risk losing it all with a single disastrous system.

Strong leadership skills will ensure that your architecture is implemented properly by the development team.

Strong Project Management Is Necessary for Success

Speaking of strong leadership, good project management is also necessary for an enterprise system project to succeed. In some small projects, one or more of the architects may perform the duties of project management, but usually there are separate project managers.

Good project managers are supporters and facilitators of the development team. They make sure the project stays on schedule, and they serve as the liaison to the overall project environment, which includes the future users, senior management, and other projects. They shield the development team members from administrative demands on their time, and sometimes they may need to resolve conflicts that may arise within the team.

In successful projects, the project managers and the system architects work closely together and coordinate their activities. A project manager may view the architects as team leaders who are in charge of the developers implementing their architecture. The project manager coordinates the work among the team leaders.

Project Milestones Are Opportunities for Demos and Rebalancing

It is absolutely essential for an enterprise system project to set milestones in the project schedule. The project managers and the system architects need to work out what and when the milestones are and then get the entire development team to agree to them.

Every milestone should include a demonstration of the capabilities of the system at that point. A demo is both a proof of concept and a proof of progress, and it verifies that the system components developed so far can work together. Demos give meaning to milestones.

Each milestone gives the project managers a chance to rebalance the workload among the development team members to ensure that they can reach the next milestone. At different times during the development cycle, some developers may get ahead, and others may fall behind. Each milestone is an opportunity to move resources to where they are needed.

At the beginning of the project, milestones should be fairly close together, and it should be relatively easy to reach from one to the next. The very first milestone should be the initial successful end-to-end thread of execution (see Figure 17-1). These early milestones help the project team calibrate the level of difficulty of the work and set the confidence level of meeting the overall schedule. Afterward, you can space the milestones farther apart. Your final milestones near the project deadline should be spaced closely and evenly, such as weekly milestones.

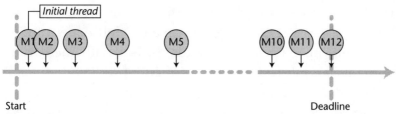

Figure 17-1: The very first project milestone should be the initial successful thread of execution through the enterprise system. The first few milestones should be spaced closely. The final milestones should be spaced closely and evenly.

The Project Milestones Near the End Allow You to Get Your Project Done on Schedule

When your project meets its milestones, you are assured that it is making forward progress. But are you confident that you will be able to get your enterprise system completed on schedule—in other words, will you get the product out the door on time?

There is nothing worse than having a project panic near the deadline and start ripping out features. These actions are unplanned, and if there are hidden dependencies among the components, removing some of them at the last minute may cripple the entire system.

Expect the schedule to slip, and plan for them up front. You can monitor the schedule slippage with the project milestones.

When you are defining the milestones, the ones near the end have special importance. The development team should agree which of them is the first one that can be a "release candidate." A release candidate is a milestone that represents the completion of minimally acceptable functionality. In your worst-case scenario, this milestone would be the product that you can release to your users as being "complete." Subsequent milestones would all be release candidates, but with increasing functionality, and thus they represent better products.

The key idea behind having your final milestones be release candidates is that the development team planned and agreed to each one ahead of time. If the schedule slips, there will be less panicking (see Figure 17-2).

Release candidate milestones also make more satisfied customers. If the development is slipping its schedule, the project managers can meet with the customers to negotiate for extra development time. The customers can weigh the costs of a delayed product and help choose which release candidate would satisfy them.

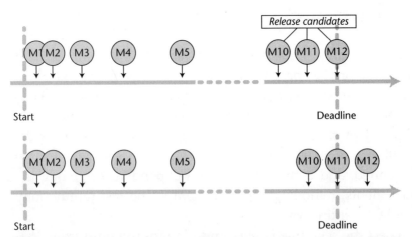

Figure 17-2: Project milestones with a schedule slip and (hopefully!) less panic at the end.

Don't ignore people issues.

Ultimately, it will be project team members that determine whether your software project will succeed or fail. Enterprise system projects tend to be larger than the average software project and involve more developers working simultaneously on different parts of the system.

Woe is any enterprise project that ignores its people issues!

Software Projects Are Not Democracies

Project members should not expect their project to be a democracy. Ideally, it should have the *appearance* of a democracy, at least in the beginning. In a well-run project, the project manager encourages all the project members to express their opinions. There will be meetings where everybody contributes ideas, and there will be discussions and arguments over the ideas. During these discussions, the ideas will mutate and evolve.

But at some point, after having taken in and considered all the input, and preferably still early in the project, the project manager and the system architects must make their decision about which way the project must go, and then they must *lead*.

There should be no secret ballots, no voting, no notion of majority rules. Instead, the project manager or the chief architect must be a dictator (hopefully benign) and tell everybody in which direction to go.

Agree to Disagree, but Then Move On

You do not want your project to hold endless design meetings to attempt to "reach consensus." Unless you are fortunate to be in a project where most of the members have worked together for a while and think alike, these meetings usually degenerate into opportunities for someone on the team to say no and hold up progress.

When the project manager or the architects make their decision, the project members may have to agree that some of them disagree with the decision, but all must agree to move forward.

It is important that tomorrow you will be at a different place in your project than where you are today. Then you can compare the two places and determine whether you are going in the right direction or whether you need to make a course correction. A project that's mired in meetings will not gain this valuable insight.

Scale the Project According to the Team Members' Abilities and Experience

The team members' abilities and experience are assets that you can nurture and grow. But when you are designing the system, you must take into account the current state of their abilities and experience.

A good architect scales the complexity of the project to the team members' abilities and experience or to that of the developers he or she can expect to hire. Of course, you can expect the team members to do some learning on the job, so you can afford to design a system that's a bit above their current capabilities to develop.

But if you go too far, the team will constantly be in research mode, and it will not make enough forward progress. The first few project milestones are a good gauge of how well suited the team is to the project as designed.

Do Not Be a Slave to the Latest Project Management Methodology

A sure sign of inexperienced or lazy project leadership is a manager who adopts a management methodology—usually the one currently written up in the trade rags and tech journals—and slavishly follows it.

At any moment, there is always a "hot" methodology that promises to make all developers productive and every project successful. In the 1970s, it was Chief Programmer Teams, and recently, it has been Extreme Programming.

You simply cannot expect to impose a project management methodology as described in a book or an article on your project team and expect it work. Every methodology has its good points and bad points. A project manager may need to examine several methodologies and find the techniques that will work with the project team members' personalities and experience levels.

Foster Good Communication Plus Teamwork, Teamwork, Teamwork

Without good communication among the project team members, especially in a project developing a complex enterprise system, teamwork will be difficult. Without good teamwork, the project will miss its milestones, and it is likely to fail completely.

There are various ways that team members can communicate with each other, such as face to face in meetings or casually in the hallways, or by e-mail, instant messaging, or phone calls. Good communication must also occur up and down the project hierarchy among the developers, architects, and project managers.

Be wary of the team member who works strange hours and never sees or communicates with the others, or the one who always telecommutes and never shows up for meetings. Project management needs to pull such people back into fold, especially if they are working on critical parts of the system upon which the rest of the team depends.

Good teamwork is a consequence of good communication. When project team members are constantly in touch with each other, they will make sure that everybody is on the same page and pulling together in the same direction.

Remove Team Members Who Cannot or Will Not Perform

A project manager has an easy job when all the project team members communicate well, they work together harmoniously, and the project continues to meet its milestones.

Unfortunately, there may be a team member who refuses to work with the others, insists on doing things his or her way, does not follow the standards established by the rest of the team, is argumentative and disruptive, or who simply just isn't capable of performing the work. This person may even have been a superstar in the recent past before joining your project.

If you are the project manager or a system architect, then you must decide if this person's contribution to the project is positive or negative. If your attempts at reforming this individual aren't working, then you must conclude that he or she simply isn't a good fit for the project and should leave. Afterward, you may discover much relief among the rest of the project team and see a rise in the level of productivity.

*Software
engineering is all
about the D's.*

Software engineering is a relatively new engineering discipline that focuses on the process of creating successful software. Success criteria include delivery on time and on budget, reliability, and, of course, satisfied users.

Much has been written on software engineering during the past few decades. Texts and articles promulgate many principles, some of which I have cast as Martian principles in this book.

For this current principle, I provide an outline of software engineering to help put the other Martian principles into proper context. This outline is a small collection of what I call the "*D*-topics" of software engineering.

Discovery

Before you can write any software to solve a problem, you first have to discover that there *is* a problem that you can solve.

If you are an enterprise system architect, or a project manager for such a project, you need to answer several important questions at the very beginning. Is the problem distributed in nature? Does it make sense to have services residing on a central server and multiple remote client applications? Are there services that ought to be shared among the clients? How crucial are accessibility, reliability, and scalability?

If you do not have good answers to such questions at the onset, then you may not have discovered an appropriate problem to solve. You could end up creating an enterprise system that nobody will need, or one that is overkill for a particular problem.

Diplomacy

Another critical question to answer in the beginning is: Can I work with the stakeholders to understand the problem and create its solution? Stakeholders are the people with a strong vested interest in your solution, and they include the future users of your enterprise system, their managers, and the people who will pay you for the software.

Working out these interpersonal relationships requires good diplomatic skills, especially on the part of the system architect. This may be a challenge if you are better at dealing with programs than with people. But if an architect and the stakeholders cannot agree on what the problem is and what kind of solution is appropriate, then the project cannot succeed.

Definition

Once the initial negotiations with the stakeholders are done, the project leaders, including the managers and the architects, must create a working project definition. The project definition includes requirements, software architectures, project schedules, resources, and personnel.

This will only be a *working* definition because, as one of the Martian principles states, most likely you will not be able to get precise requirements at this point. As you do rapid prototyping and engage in give-and-take with the future users, the requirements will converge and the project definition will solidify.

Design

All things considered, software architecture is mainly about design. Many of the Martian principles are indeed design principles.

The software engineering discipline prescribes many methodologies for doing good software design. As one of the Martian principles warns, do not slavishly follow any one methodology, but be flexible and adapt the best techniques from among the methodologies to suit your particular project.

Software design should remain primarily a *creative* activity that is guided by sound principles.

Development

A software design for an enterprise system is worthless if you cannot build the system. Several of the Martian principles are about development.

Code development is a highly dynamic activity. But remember that the major challenges are not in writing the code but in integrating the components into a working system. As stated by the principles, strong project leadership, clear schedule milestones, and a proper build environment are all important.

Debugging

Debugging an enterprise system can be much more difficult than debugging a standalone application. Not only are the software components distributed, but they can also interact with each other in nondeterministic ways. Temporarily setting a breakpoint or inserting a "print" statement can affect interaction timing—a bug may show up only when you are not looking for it!

Several of the Martian principles offer suggestions for debugging, such as inserting permanent monitoring hooks into the code or logging. If the middleware services are independent of each other, then it will be easier to test and debug them separately.

Documentation

Documentation must include both user documentation and procedures for the system operators and maintainers. It can range from bound manuals with illustrations to simple "how to" one-pagers.

Projects often leave writing documentation until the very end. Ideally, the writers should begin shortly before the system components are tested. It is not unusual for the writers to become testers as they try out the features they are documenting.

If you find that a system component or feature is difficult to explain in the documentation, it may be that the software itself was not designed well.

Deployment

Once you have built the enterprise system, how will you deploy it? Enterprise systems are usually complex and consist of many components. If you cannot deploy it reliably, it will not matter how well it was designed and built.

Make sure your architecture results in software that you can deploy. The Martian principles involving hot-redeployable components and maintaining a separate build and deployment environment are important.

Dmaintenance

Ah, yes, dmaintenance! Your enterprise system has an operational life after deployment. Once your system is up and running, how will you keep it going despite changes and new requirements?

Make sure that your architecture follows the Martian principles on maintenance, such as using parameter files and creating dynamically reconfigurable plug-and-play services. If your services are independent of each other, you will be able to shut them down one at a time if necessary for maintenance, while keeping the other services and the system as a whole running.

The formulas for success aren't complicated.

We can summarize this book with two simple formulas. But just because a formula is simple does not mean that it is trivial or superficial. After all, Einstein's $e = mc^2$ looks pretty simple, but few would claim that what it represents is trivial.

Successful Architect = Good Designer + Good Developer + Good Leader

Not long ago, I was invited by an industry group to participate in a panel discussion before an audience of software developers. The panelists were all software architects, and the topic was "What do software architects do?".

During the discussion, I was a bit dismayed to hear that several of the other panelists thought it was possible to be a good architect even if all you did was design, and you left the implementations to others. They must be far better architects than I am. In my experience, I have succeeded only when I have been involved with most, if not all, of the software engineering D-topics.

In my opinion, the most successful architects are good designers, and they are good developers, and they are good leaders. Leadership is important to guide the rest of the development team to adhere to the Martian principles and to drive the project to success.

Successful System = Good Architecture + Good Software Engineering

The Martian principles are about software architecture and software engineering. If you do well on both, your enterprise system will be a success.

Keep It Simple!

Developing an enterprise system is already a very complicated business. Do not make it worse. Keep everything as simple as you can, even if that means implementing minimal functionality.

If you have a simple-as-possible system up and running, you will find the time to add appropriate functionality wherever necessary. On the other hand, if you have an overly complex system that does not work, you will never have enough time to fix it.

So, keep it simple!

Index